Grace of line,

play of light

and shade,

balance of color,

discretion in

adornment

Grace of line,

play of light

and shade,

balance of color,

discretion in

adornment

The Cathedral
At the Heart of Los Angeles

Michael Downey

Photography by Tom Bonner
Design by Greg Becker

LITURGICAL PRESS

Introduction

A book *for* the heart. Words and images summon the ear and the eye of the heart. No pages of history, lists of facts, or detailed descriptions here. Instead, an invitation to journey in, with, and to the Light. Photos taken as the Cathedral was nearing completion give glimpses of a work of the people still in progress.

At the heart of Los Angeles, the Cathedral evokes *from* the human heart its deepest longings and desires, reminding us of what we are called to be and to become. It stirs to sprouting again the seed of our hope that all men and women might one day share in the life and goodness of a world created and blessed by God:

"My house shall be called a house of prayer for all peoples." (Isaiah 56:7)

> ***For** the heart,*
>
> > ***from** the heart,*
> >
> > > ***to** the heart of this Cathedral:*
> > >
> > > > *the Mother Church of Los Angeles*
> > > >
> > > > *called Our Lady of the Angels*
> > > >
> > > > *a place of gathering*
> > > >
> > > > *of light and of journey*
> > > >
> > > > *with room enough for all.*

The Cathedral of Our Lady of the Angels

Beauty courses through her very being. Everything about her is sincere, open, honest. Grace of line, play of light and shade, balance of color, discretion in adornment: Our Lady of the Angels. The Cathedral at the heart of Los Angeles, the soul and center of Southern California.

Cement and tile and stone and marble and alabaster and wood. The talents of architects and craftspeople and artists. The sweat of construction workers and the generous gifts of people from near and far. The labor of many years, shaped by a guiding vision. If all we had here was simply a serenely lovely building, we would most certainly have failed in our task, squandered the offer of a lifetime. But what we have is something that is so much more, a gift that surpasses and confounds all our words. Behold, Beauty's dwelling: wholeness, harmony, radiance.

Here the whole people of the Archdiocese of Los Angeles, from Hollywood and Compton, from Beverly Hills and Watts, from Santa Barbara and San Pedro, from San Gabriel and San Fernando, from Koreatown and East LA, the rich and poor from all ways and walks of life, have pooled what they have to make a place that belongs to all of us, with room enough for everyone, a place for everything that ennobles the human spirit: fine art, music, folk craft, worship, and more. The Cathedral, no matter how splendid it might be, is simply a setting for the most precious of jewels—God's people, in all their diversity.

Only the words beyond and beneath words, the language of poetry, come close to expressing what we have here. For we have raised up something that will elude all our efforts to pin it down and say precisely: *This* is what the Cathedral of Our Lady of the Angels is. And *this* is what it is for. From age to age, season to season, gathering to gathering, Sunday to Sunday, procession to procession, celebration to celebration, this space, this place, will all at once hold and offer us more meanings than any of us can ever know. Over and over again it will be more than what it is, summoning us to so much more than we ever dreamed we might be. For this Cathedral at the heart of Los Angeles and its people is itself more than we ever dreamed it might be.

In an age whose greatest poverty may be its service to the literal, to the purely functional, the Cathedral's testament to the vitality of poetry in light may be its greatest achievement. The place invites contemplative moments: pondering and gazing, lingering and beholding so that we might discover the presence of the living God in the simple act of looking long and lovingly.

Structure and adornment, spaces both open and enclosed, thin clean lines of shadow, shafts and shades of light, texture both sumptuous and spare—all these invite the eye of the heart to behold the beauty of God not only in visual delight, but also in the awareness of what is missing, in the draw of the human heart beyond what is here.

Music and movement, gesture and action, word and silence are also at play. This is a place where there is room for words to be spoken and sung in a way that allows the Word, the Love of God who comes and is coming, to spring forth beneath and beyond the words. Here we discover in simple elements—bread, wine, water, and oil—the presence of God's life among us. Here are harmonies and gradations of texture, of touch, of scent, of sound, of light that stir up in us and evoke from us honesty, simplicity, and reverence.

Here we come to know the simple truth: Not only is God in us— we are in God! From age to age, Christians have built places where people can find God and know themselves to be *in God by being in these places.*

We know that we are *in God* when we are in this place: The Cathedral at the heart of the City of the Angels.

O wisdom's jewel

Glow, no shine! and shatter the darkness of our night.

O seat of brilliant light

Your shimmering floods night's sky.

O Light's never-ending ember

Let the rays of your dawn kiss our eyes.

O house of Jacob,

come, let us walk

in the light of the Lord!

(Isaiah 2:5)

A Church with a Chair

A cathedral is the center of life in the local Church. The very word "cathedral," in Latin or Greek, means "chair." From the *cathedra*, the chair or seat, the bishop teaches, sanctifies, and guides the People of God, the Church. From the cathedral, the church with the bishop's chair, the bishop oversees and safeguards the life of the Catholic people.

Since the early Christian centuries, while seated in their chairs and facing their people, bishops have preached the Gospel of Christ to them. Respect for the chair, the *cathedra,* has always signified respect for the bishop and for his sanctifying and governing role, for his role as teacher and witness to Christ.

In the Cathedral of Our Lady of the Angels is seated the Archbishop of Los Angeles—of the whole of Los Angeles and all of its people. His title signals the pastoral care and responsibility he has for each and every person in this widespread city of many cities, and especially for the wounded and the weak, the last, the littlest, and the least.

There is a chair in every diocese, in every local Church. From his chair the bishop gathers the people, like a shepherd bringing together a flock. He instructs, encourages, sometimes admonishes, but always challenges them. It is here that the people drink of the rich reserves of the Catholic tradition. And it is here that the mystery at the heart of the Catholic faith—the mystery of Christ himself present and active through the gift of the Spirit—is celebrated in its fullness.

The Body of Christ, the Church, comes to full stature when its members gather for prayer and worship together with their bishop, his presbyters, deacons, and other ministers at the altar, united to every other local Church in the world and to the Bishop of Rome as their head. It is here that the unity of the Church becomes visible. This is the prime expression of the Church as *one, holy, catholic,* and *apostolic*, the marks of the Church affirmed week by week as the Catholic people throughout the world profess the Creed together. Every bishop's ministry is to preserve communion—the bonds of

faith, hope, and love—among all those who come together at the Table of Word and Sacrament as Christians have done from the time of the apostles.

Gathered by Word and Sacrament with our bishop as the one Body of Christ, we are in the presence of the Apostolic Church here and now. The Spirit evokes the Apostolic Church not by bringing us into the past, but by wedding the past to the faith and life of this community in the present. The gifts of the Spirit are enlivened and fully flourish in a way that marked the early gatherings of the Church at prayer. Thus we move forward to the future. The cathedral becomes the Church *par excellence* when the Catholic faithful are gathered in all their diversity for prayer and worship together with their bishop and the ministers of Christ and the Church.

A cathedral is, above all, a house for the Church. It must be a fitting place, worthy of the mysteries celebrated and received in it. It is to be high enough, lean and spare enough, so that the eye and the heart are lifted to God. It is to be wide enough to welcome all who come, believers and unbelievers, people who belong to the Catholic community and those who don't. The cathedral is to invite all of us to a future full of hope and promise even while keeping our minds and hearts rooted in the truth that has been handed on to us from generation to generation, like God's mercy rolling down the ages.

The Cathedral of Our Lady of the Angels serves as a luminous link to our past. It is a building of breadth and breath, braiding living bonds between men and women of today and the riches of a glorious heritage. Through stone and glass, cement and tile, marble and wood, space and sound, the Cathedral grounds us in our history, so that we can face the changes and challenges of our age and move with courage into the future.

Standing in this place, the heart remembers. The earth quaked. Walls were shaken. The mountains rocked. The Spirit stirred. A time came to move on, to leave behind what once was for what might be. The hour came for leading the way, for giving shape to a vision and for surrendering to it, following over higher hurdles and down more verdant paths than we ever could have imagined to this space—high and wide and bright—with room enough for the constant coming of the Light in our midst.

O send out your light and your truth;

   let them lead me;

let them bring me to your holy hill

   and to your dwelling.

(Psalm 43:3)

A Place for a People

Whether it be majestic or modest, spare or sumptuous, a cathedral's worth cannot be measured. A cathedral is a place for people. They are drawn by a cathedral's quiet, taken in by the peace of the place, held in its strength and embraced by its lavish simplicity.

A cathedral is a place where the human heart and its deepest longings can find rest. For a moment. For we are on the move, a people on the way. We have here no final resting place. Yet, at times of gathering and celebration, for prayer and intercession, for praise and blessing, or if only for a brief time of silence, for a quiet pause, we come here to the Cathedral, amidst life's journey.

Here in this place we are bathed in light, God's own light shattering the darkness of our lives, bringing warmth to hearts frozen stiff with apathy, enlightening the eye of the heart to gaze on one and all with the light of God's love streaming through us.

If we allow it, the light caressing the walls and wideness of this space can flood every inch and ounce of our living. Stilled and strengthened by the gift of God's life and love received and celebrated in this place and its people, we can take up again life's journey with all its hopes and disappointments, longings and struggles, heartbreaks and joys. We can move onward until, at the end of our life's journey, we breathe our last, having been led by the light of Christ to the fullness of Light.

O time of God appointed

O bright and holy morn,

By your constant coming in light,

Bring us life again.

Learn where there is wisdom,
where there is strength,
where there is understanding,
so that you may at the same time discern
where there is length of days, and life,
where there is light for the eyes, and peace.
(Baruch 3:14)

To Gather the Church

The Cathedral, the heart of Los Angeles, is an architectural hymn that swells in praise and thanksgiving for the endless variation, subtlety, and complexity of the human journey. It is a place for conducting the transactions of Christian life. But here everything given and received lies within an economy of gift—all that is given and received is gift. The Cathedral is the site for an exchange of the gifts that have been and are being given by God to a people, God's Holy People, the Church.

It is in the Cathedral that the Catholic community does what is central to its faith and life: welcoming the newborn, celebrating the Eucharist, pronouncing vows, commending the dead to the Lord, preaching the word, ordaining and commissioning for ministry, discussing the theological issues of our day, teaching with authority, educating the children, organizing the work to be done in the wider world, hosting banquets, gathering what is needed for the poor, supporting the oppressed, and opening doors to those rejected elsewhere. Many of these exchanges go on at the very same time.

And so, the Cathedral is never idle. This haven of quiet and contemplation is also an arena for conducting the activities of faith, of hope, of love—a place poised at the center of community life, both sacred and secular. Flowing out from the silence at the heart of the Cathedral there is always the humming of a wide range of activities harmonious with the Church's mission to be a living sign of reconciliation and peace, of joy and of hope for the people of our age.

In this place, God's people made holy by being brought into the Body of Christ gather for prayer and praise. Some are commissioned for various ministries in the local Church. Here catechists listen to the word of God and are sent forth to teach as Jesus did. In this place some are ordained to the order of presbyter and of deacon, and priests gather with their bishop for the Chrism Mass to receive from his hands the consecrated oils for their ministry of healing. Here the sacraments of initiation are celebrated in their fullness during the Easter Vigil. It is in the Cathedral that the people hear the call to repentance and forgiveness, and the challenge to ongoing, lifelong conversion. It is from this place that lay missionaries are sent to different parts of the world to spread the Gospel, a message of faith so full and whole that it stretches out and pours itself forth in lives of service to other peoples in other lands.

The Cathedral opens up a vision beyond its own walls and borders, impelling all who come to go now and pass on to others the gift that has been received in and from this place.

One and all

great and small

coming from every race, land, and language

we are

Your Body living and breathing in our own time and place.

We live, move, and have our being

through you, with you, in you.

Washed in the waters of baptism

strengthened in the Spirit's anointing

sustained season by season

    week by week,

    day by day

    by a morsel of heaven's bread and a swallow of true vine's precious gift.

We live and breathe in one Love

becoming Love itself speaking in a fleshly way.

Through the glance of an eye

    by the touch of a hand

        in this word of comfort

            or that little cup of cold water given in your name.

You are in our midst

dwelling here among us.

But you have come to Mount Zion and to the city of the living God,

the heavenly Jerusalem,

and to innumerable angels in festal gathering . . .

(Hebrews 12:22)

With Room Enough for All

The Cathedral of Our Lady of the Angels brings new life and energy to the heart of the city, transforming the City of the Angels and its people by reminding us, inspiring us, evoking from us a deep awareness of what this city is, what it is called to be. The Cathedral is a symbol of our future together, calling all of us to everything that is good and noble in human life, inviting all of us to fulfill our longing for truth, for goodness, for beauty.

The Cathedral is the center of the life and prayer of the Catholic people. But it also speaks to all the people of Los Angeles, the earthly city stretching beyond itself, reaching for more, straining onward and upward toward the completion yet to come in the new Jerusalem. The Cathedral reminds us of our deepest hungers, evokes our greatest hopes, calls forth our desire for all that is best in us, stirs up in our hearts reserves of anticipation for what is yet to come. The sound of its bells, its grand façade, alabaster windows, wide and welcoming nave take us beyond our narrow vision and invite us to what is wider, broader, higher, and deeper than ourselves.

The Cathedral is a place, a focus, a resource, but, above all, it is an icon in cement and alabaster, marble and wood and stone raised up for all peoples, a prophetic word written in architecture—a word that will speak to generations for hundreds of years. It is a sign that sings of the Church's ongoing commitment to the city, an image of how people of every race, land, and language might come together and live as one family in a world transformed by self-giving love. Especially when the Catholic faithful are gathered in all their diversity for prayer and worship together with their bishop and ministers, the Cathedral is the Church alive, a vibrant sacrament of light, life, and love in and for the world.

As a place of gathering, of convocation, of encounter with the living God, the Cathedral is a house of worship for the Church of Los Angeles, and a house of prayer for all peoples. But, just as much, it is the place from which we are sent forth to be and to build the new Jerusalem in our midst. It is where the deepest aspirations of every human heart, indeed the longings of the whole people of a city, find a place. It is a seedbed of hope that our deepest longings will be met in the fullness of time.

The icon shimmers, the symbol sings when it is enlivened by the Spirit, moving like a mighty wind through the hearts of the People of God who gather for worship within the Cathedral's walls. For it is not just the building, sumptuous or spare, that makes a cathedral. It is the living faith, the abundant hope, and the flourishing of love among the People of God who gather here that allows the icon to illuminate, the symbol to swell in a song of the new heaven, the new earth, the new Jerusalem.

In the end, the Cathedral is nothing more, or less, than a house for all people who pray, a house for the Church, a home for the Body of Christ—member for member—called to become a living doxology, a continual act of praise and thanksgiving both here, within these walls, and beyond. If the Cathedral is a setting for a precious gem, and its people the jewel, then their gathering for prayer and worship is the moment when their refulgence streams forth in all its brilliance.

"Then I saw a new heaven and a new earth; for the first heaven and the first earth had passed away, and the sea was no more. And I saw the holy city, the new Jerusalem, coming down out of heaven from God, prepared as a bride adorned for her husband. And I heard a loud voice from the throne saying, 'See, the home of God is among mortals. He will dwell with them; they will be his peoples, and God himself will be with them; he will wipe every tear from their eyes. Death will be no more; mourning and crying and pain will be no more, for the first things have passed away.'" (Revelation 21:1–4)

The light shines in the darkness, and the darkness
did not overcome it.
(John 1:5)

A Place of Light

All life long we are learning how to see. Life in Christ is a way of seeing by loving, and loving by seeing. The more we see, the more we love. And the more we love, the more we learn how to see with new eyes, the eyes of the heart.

Light, color, harmony, and balance. Light invites passage into a world a-shimmer. Here we gaze upon shades of reflectivity, the subtle way in which each element, every particle of creation, responds to the touch of light's generous and gentle fingers. If only for a moment, we glimpse and are drawn in by the lavish everyday doings of light, an ordinary, oft-taken-for-granted blessing. The extravagant abundance of such a gift allows us to peer into the near-miraculous in the utterly plain, seeing the grandeur in the gritty, the holy in the humdrum, the sanctity in the city.

The light within moves us and draws us beyond these walls, and over the higher walls of our frozen hearts. Because the Cathedral is a place of openness and light, its walls are porous, its gates gossamer. There are no longer two cities—the City of God and the City of the Human Family. There is one city, whose citizens gather here and are sent forth from here, to prepare for the coming of the day of the Lord, for a new heaven and a new earth. Here, in this place, we glimpse traces of a world transformed. In the blink of an eye: a new creation seized and saturated by God's own light.

Self-effacing

whisper of Life,

by your light we see Light.

First glimpsed in a crib,

Raised up on a cross—

    Love swaddled and then stretched to breaking,

    breathing and speaking a Love broader than earth's bounds.

Love's looking

in the living icon of the Father's face,

    seen and touched by a heart awakened by Life's Light.

Gaze, then, long and lovingly

upon the One who is here and there,

all at once and all ways enlightening, enlivening, guiding, comforting

    yet hardest to see or hear.

Spirit, Holy Spirit, Spirit of God, Spirit of Christ

    O self-effacing One.

You who are the silence of Love's never-ending gaze,

You who have guided my life until this day so that still I live,

    Speak, whisper, just one word,

And in the darkness of night I shall see again

    the Light which is your Life.

A Place to Journey Together

They have gone before us. Their names echo from centuries past: Andrew, Agatha, Bonaventure, Bernadette, Charles, Cecilia, Philomena, Paul, Thomas, Teresa. We remember the lives and legacies of those who sowed and strengthened the seeds of faith on this land: Junipero Serra, Elizabeth Ann Seton, Katharine Drexel, Kateri Tekakwitha, Philippine Duchesne, John Neumann. In our own day the saints among us call us to pour out our lives in service and thanks to God, becoming together with them a living sacrifice of praise in word and deed.

They walk beside us—on each side of us. The saints. They come from every age, land and language. They are teachers and preachers, bishops and theologians, ministers of mercy and those who nurse the blind and lame. They are called "Sister" and "Brother," they are religious and worldly, wounded and weak, wealthy and indigent, cleric and lay, busy and prayerful, young and old. Some of the saints are not recognized as such: ordinary people in heaven, saints nonetheless. Their hearts and hands have been given to God in days of toil and in hours of ease—by God's gift, not by their own doing. We look to them so that we too might be more like the Christ whose name we bear.

For your holy ones there was very great light.

(Wisdom 18:1)

They call us forward, for they have gone ahead. They beckon and we follow, and together we move closer in the light, to the Light. And they wait for us as we continue on the journey through this life to the fullness of the life they now taste.

Through their words, we have heard the very speech of God. Through their deeds we have seen love in flesh in every age. Through their acts of mercy and compassion, they have awakened in us our longing for God. They do this now as they surround us: a great cloud of witnesses.

They encourage us and pray for us. And they receive our prayers, joining our prayers to their never-ending prayer to the Father through Christ in the Spirit, asking God's favor on us and those whom we love. For our needs, both great and small, we pray. To the holy women and men, those who are blessed, those who are saints, we pray. For the poor, the hungry, and the sick, we pray. For peace and reconciliation among families, nations, races, and classes, we pray. In thanksgiving for our health and for the gift of family and friendship, we pray. For our civic and religious leaders, we pray. Joined with them in one communion, the communion of saints, the living and the dead, those in glory and those of us still on the way, we become one Body, one Spirit, in Christ. Together with all the saints.

We are held and helped and made strong now by their prayer in that blessed communion. All of us, the living and the dead, are drawn ever more fully into love's flourishing. And in the bond stronger than death we raise our voices, gently or in jubilation, invoking their names:

James
Charles Borromeo
Catherine of Siena
Isaac Jogues
Joan of Arc

Barnabas
Jane Frances de Chantal
Anthony Claret
Methodius
Cyril of Jerusalem
Pius X

Andrew Dung Lac
Aloysius Gonzaga
Marie-Rose Durocher
Stephen of Hungary
Matthew
Young Women of Faith

John
Lorenzo Ruiz
Philippine Duchesne
John Baptist Scalabrini
Joseph Vaz

Justin
Margaret of Scotland
Helen
Louise de Marillac
Emydius

Philip
John Bosco
Mary of Jesus Crucified
Francis de Sales
Philomena

	Pray for us
	Pray for us
	Pray for us
	Pray for us
	Pray for us
	Pray for us
	Pray for us
	Pray for us
	Pray for us
	Pray for us
	Pray for us
	Pray for us
	Pray for us
	Pray for us
	Pray for us
	Pray for us
	Pray for us
	Pray for us
	Pray for us
	Pray for us
	Pray for us
	Pray for us
	Pray for us
	Pray for us
	Pray for us
	Pray for us
	Pray for us
	Pray for us
	Pray for us
	Pray for us
	Pray for us
	Pray for us

John XXIII	Pray for us
Mother Teresa	Pray for us
Bartholomew	Pray for us
Anselm	Pray for us
Bruno	Pray for us
Maria de la Cabeza	Pray for us
Isidore the Farmworker	Pray for us
John Fisher	Pray for us
Junipero Serra	Pray for us
Mark	Pray for us
John Neumann	Pray for us
Alphonsus Liguori	Pray for us
Bede	Pray for us
Agnes	Pray for us
Andrew Kim Taegon	Pray for us
John Vianney	Pray for us
Martin of Porres	Pray for us
Boniface	Pray for us
Justin de Jacobis	Pray for us
Children of God	Pray for us
Bridget of Sweden	Pray for us
Vincent de Paul	Pray for us
Bernadette	Pray for us
Elizabeth of Hungary	Pray for us
Ambrose	Pray for us
Gregory the Great	Pray for us

Juan Diego	Pray for us
Martin of Tours	Pray for us
Teresa of Avila	Pray for us
Alojzije Stepinac	Pray for us
Jacinta	Pray for us
Patrick	Pray for us
Francis Xavier	Pray for us
John Chrysostom	Pray for us
Frances X. Cabrini	Pray for us
Young Men of Faith	Pray for us
Jerome	Pray for us
Rose of Lima	Pray for us
Lucy	Pray for us
Blaise	Pray for us
Anthony of Padua	Pray for us
Martha	Pray for us
Philip Neri	Pray for us
Timothy	Pray for us
Benedict the Black	Pray for us
Luke	Pray for us
Lucia Khambang	Pray for us

JUAN DIEGO   MARTIN OF TOURS   TERESA OF AVILA

ALOJZIJE STEPINAC

PATRICK

JACINTA

Perpetua	Pray for us
Felicitas	Pray for us
Andrew	Pray for us
Peter Claver	Pray for us
Bonaventure	Pray for us
Andre Bessette	Pray for us
Elizabeth of Portugal	Pray for us
Elizabeth Ann Seton	Pray for us
Mothers and Children of Grace	Pray for us

Paul	Pray for us	Joseph
Peter	Pray for us	Ann
Charles Lwanga	Pray for us	Mary Magdalen
Maria Goretti	Pray for us	Dominic
Agatha	Pray for us	Nicholas
Miguel Agustin Pro	Pray for us	Thomas More
Lawrence	Pray for us	Kateri Tekakwitha
Louis Ibaraki	Pray for us	Moses the Ethiopian
Paul Miki	Pray for us	Paul Chong Hasang
Therese of Lisieux	Pray for us	John Baptist de la Salle
Jurgis Matulaitis	Pray for us	Maximilian Kolbe
Bernard	Pray for us	John of God
Augustine	Pray for us	Katharine Drexel
John the Baptist	Pray for us	Thomas Aquinas
Maria Venegas	Pray for us	Bernardine of Siena
Peter Chanel	Pray for us	Frances of Rome
Thomas	Pray for us	Ignatius of Loyola
Monica	Pray for us	Casimir
Clare	Pray for us	Stephen
Francis of Assisi	Pray for us	Cecilia

Pray for us
Pray for us
Pray for us
Pray for us
Pray for us

Pray for us
Pray for us
Pray for us
Pray for us
Pray for us

Pray for us
Pray for us
Pray for us
Pray for us
Pray for us

Pray for us
Pray for us
Pray for us
Pray for us
Pray for us

CECILIA STEPHEN CASIMIR IGNATIUS FRANCES
OF OF
LOYOLA ROME

She is a reflection of eternal light,

a spotless mirror of the working of God.

(Wisdom 7:26)

The Place of Mary

Mary. Full of grace. The gift of God's own life pulses through the fabric of her being and is given to us through her.

She was a young woman of faith, one of the people, *indígena*, of earthen color, a girl of modest means. No. Poor.

An angel came to her. In response she gave herself to God fully, without reserve, with boundless confidence: "Let it be done as you say."

The Spirit of God overshadowed her. God's breath, God's own life and love, came to rest on her, and—through her—has come among us.

Her "yes" made all the difference. Through her, God entered the human family, became flesh of our flesh, embracing human life and the whole of our history. And through him, God in flesh, Jesus the Word of God, the human family shares in the very life of God.

In her song of joy, her Magnificat, she whom all generations call blessed gives glory to God:

My soul magnifies the Lord,
and my spirit rejoices in God my Savior . . .
For the Mighty One has done great things for me
and holy is God's name. . . .

God has brought down the powerful from their thrones
and lifted up the lowly.
God has filled the hungry with good things
and sent the rich away empty.

A woman of flesh and blood, Mary is now among the angels, yet surpassing them in grace and dignity. She calls God "my son." And God's very Word, Jesus the Son, calls her "Mother."

She is clothed in the sun. Her Son now lives in glory, raised to life without end with the One he called "Father." And the woman is there with her Son, at his side. Faithful to him in his living and his dying, from the crib and through the cross, she is first among those of the human family to taste the fullness of the divine life.

The whole of her mystery rests in a word: *"Fiat."* "Yes." By it, she became the Mother of God. And us.

Pray for us, Holy Mary, Mother of God and our mother

now and at the hour of our death.

Where you are is where we hope to be at the end of this, our life's journey.

Let us behold for all time beyond time the glory of God,

> *whose face we have seen,*

> *whose hands have healed us,*

> *whose heart was pierced and still overflowed with compassion*

because of the flesh given him by your "Yes" to the Spirit overshadowing you.

And us.

Then your light shall break forth like the dawn.

(Isaiah 58:8)

Nuestra Señora de los Angeles

There is a story to every name. From age to age the name of Mary, Miriam of Nazareth, has been invoked: Notre Dame, Nuestra Señora, Our Lady. And, through the centuries, that name has graced the houses of God.

The warm texture, the soothing, sun-caressed finish of her Cathedral lights up in mind's eye the *adobe* of the peoples who once made a home here. It was they who heard the Gospel message brought to them by the sons of Francis of Assisi. When Franciscans built a frontier outpost in this place they called it Nuestra Señora de Los Angeles de Portiuncula, in memory of Francis's little church, his "little portion," the Portiuncula, in Assisi. There Francis met to pray with his first friars, his first "little brothers"—at the Portiuncula, the church of Santa Maria degli Angeli, Holy Mary, Our Lady of the Angels. And from Santa Maria degli Angeli, the Portiuncula, Francis sent his friars out bearing good news. They have gone to peoples of every nation and language. Crossing oceans and mountains, Junipero Serra and companions came to this place in the sun. To sow the seeds of a living Gospel.

Those who have dwelt here, from that day to this, have been named for her. We are el Pueblo de Nuestra Señora de Los Angeles de Portiuncula. Los Angelinos, the people of Los Angeles. This city of many cities is hers. This is her Cathedral. And it is ours.

Wherever she is, the angels are near. They surround her as she leads us to where she now lives in the fullness of God's promise. And, with her, the angels join in unceasing praise: Holy, Holy, Holy is the Lord God. They are messengers, conduits, companions, guardians, heralds, protectors. They intercede for us. They are called Michael, Gabriel, Raphael. Their names and number are beyond telling and counting. They live in ceaseless praise of God.

But they come to us. They bring comfort and they challenge us, as Gabriel did Mary, bringing frightening, wondrous news. They hover near, bringing a message of peace to all people of good will, as they did at the beginning on that holy night in Bethlehem when Mary gave flesh to God through her own flesh. And at the end, an angel bathed in light, his appearance like lightning. The message: "Do not be afraid. I know that you are seeking Jesus the crucified. He has been raised, just as he said." Our life in Christ by the gift of the Spirit to the glory of God the Father. It begins with the message of an angel: The Crucified One lives!

And they now wait for us. Beckoning us. Whispering: "Come." "Draw near." "To the crib." "To the cross." "In the beginning." "At the end."

Beginnings and endings. All connected. Everything is related to everything else in the circle of God's love. The earth, the highest heavens, the stars and planets and galaxies, the living and the dead, saints and sinners, angels and archangels, the lofty and the little—all live and move and have their being from the same source who is Life, Light, and Love.

Hover near us

> *those who come to this place.*

Speak a good word,

> *so that we might be an encouraging word in the world.*

Guard us in the shadow of your wings,

> *so that our shattered spirits may soar once more.*

Wait for us,

> *so that we might one day gaze with you on what you now see.*

Pray for us, with us,

> *that the woman clothed in the sun might help us to echo*

> *her "Yes" from our deepmost part,*

> *and so become, like her, bearers of God's own life.*

A Prayer in this Place

We greet you, Our Lady of the Angels

Mary, mother of grace,

And we bless your Son,

    who is God's love for us, with us.

Mother of God and mother of all

You are

    more resplendent than the cherubim

    more luminous than the seraphim.

O woman whose beauty is radiant with the quickening of the Spirit,

You have given us the ageless Word of God.

The Spirit knits in your body

    Love's own Life, who becomes our kin

God kneads in your flesh

    The leaven of the kingdom, and becomes our bread.

Eve renewed,

    Help us to walk in the light of Christ

    in whom we are made new.

Acknowledgments

My first word of thanks goes to Cardinal Roger Mahony for inviting me to convey the spirituality of the Cathedral in word and image. For entrusting this and many other tasks to me, I am grateful beyond telling.

I could not imagine a more congenial collaboration than the one I have enjoyed with Tom Bonner. What a delight it is to work with a photographer who looks and sees with the eye of a contemplative.

Monsignor Terrance Fleming provided invaluable assistance, as has Brother Hilarion O'Connor and his staff.

At the Cathedral, Monsignor Kevin Kostelnik, Pastor, welcomed me time and again as I was preparing this volume. My thanks to Isabel Loriente, Terry Casaus, and Hans Dakhlia.

Peter Dwyer at the Liturgical Press has been an ally and a trusted resource throughout. I would also like to express my thanks to Greg Becker and Ann Blattner.

A word of thanks is also offered to Eileen Bonaduce, Executive Coordinator to the Cardinal, whose efficiency and good cheer help make it possible for me to teach, research, and write from three desks while serving the Archdiocese as the Cardinal's Theologian.

Finally, my brothers at Mepkin Abbey provide both hearth and hope over the years and across the miles.

Michael Downey
Cardinal's Theologian
Archdiocese of Los Angeles

*Design and art from the Cathedral of Our Lady of the Angels
depicted in this book:*
(Unless otherwise noted, photographs are by Tom Bonner)

Design Architect: José Rafael Moneo

Executive Architect: Leo A Daly Company

General Contractor: Morley Construction Company

Liturgical and Public Art Consultant: Reverend Richard S. Vosko

Altar, *shown on title page and page 43:* Cardinal Roger Mahony

Altar Angels, *shown on title page:* M. L. Snowden

Crucifix, *shown on page 2:* Simon Toparousky
Organ: Lynn A. Dobson (Photograph by Frantisek Zvardon)

Our Lady of Guadalupe (in talavera), *shown on page 6:* Lalo Garcia

Cathedra (Chair), *shown on page 10:* Jefferson Tortorelli

Tapestry of the New Jerusalem, *shown behind chair on page 10:* John Nava

Page 12 (Photograph by Hans Dakhlia)

Page 14 (Photograph by Reuters/Landov)

Tapestry of the Baptism of the Lord, *shown on page 16:* John Nava

Tapestries of the Communion of Saints, *shown on pages 28–33:* John Nava

Great Bronze Doors, Our Lady of the Angels,
details shown on pages 34 and 40: Robert Graham

Angel Dedication Candle Holder, *shown on page 42:* Max DeMoss
(Photograph by Khoa Mai)

Altar, *page 43* (Photograph by Jim Ruymen/Reuters/Landov)

Bronze Tabernacle, *shown on page 44:* Max DeMoss
(Photograph by Khoa Mai)

Many other artists, designers, and artisans have helped to create the
Cathedral of Our Lady of the Angels.

Michael Downey is Professor of Systematic Theology
and Spirituality at Saint John's Seminary, and the
Cardinal's Theologian, Archdiocese of Los Angeles.

Tom Bonner is a photographer based in Los Angeles,
specializing in architectural subjects.

Greg Becker is a graphic designer who lives
in St. Cloud, Minnesota.

Published by Liturgical Press, Collegeville, Minnesota.

Printed in the United States of America.

ISBN 0-8146-2892-3

We know
that we are
in God
when we
are in this
place

We know

that we are

in God

when we

are in this

place